Captain Mike Ambrose,
TV weatherman and grunion hunter

Captain Mike's
COMPLETE GUIDE TO
GRUNION
HUNTING
BY
MIKE AMBROSE
AND NORA SCOTT
WALKER
ILLUSTRATIONS BY
JOHNNY HAWK
COMPLETE GUIDE TO GRUNION HUNTING
AMBROSE/WALKER

Captain Mike's Complete Guide to GRUNION HUNTING

OAK TREE

Captain Mike's Complete Guide to GRUNION HUNTING

by
Mike Ambrose
and
Nora Scott Walker

Illustrated by
Johnny Hawk

Human characters in this
book are purely fictional. Any
semblance of reality would sure surprise
the heck out of the authors.

© 1981

Captain Mike's Complete Guide to Grunion Hunting copyright © 1981 by Mike Ambrose and Nora Scott Walker. Illustrations copyright © 1981 by Johnny Hawk.

All rights reserved under International and Pan American Copyright Conventions. No part of this book may be reproduced in any manner whatsoever without written permission from the publisher, except in the case of brief quotations embodied in reviews and articles.

First Edition
Manufactured in the United States of America

For information write to:
Oak Tree Publications, Inc.
P.O. Box 1012
La Jolla, California 92038

ISBN 0-916392-70-8

1 2 3 4 5 6 7 8 9   84 83 82 81

Table of Contents

Catching the California Crazies 11
Grunion Runs, 1981-83 44-46
The Catch to Catching Grunion 47
Cooking Your Catch 82
A Word From Our Spawn-sor 84
Grunion Watchers' Report Form 90
About the Author 93
About the Other Culprits 94

Catching the California Crazies

It all started during a visit to my ancestral homeland—Handley, Texas. I arrived just in time for the gala cultural event of the season, the Annual Thespian Festival and Chili Bake-Off. For old times' sake (and because a very pushy ten-year-old insisted), I bought a ticket to *Hamlet*. Seat 13-G turned out to be only two rows behind Suzie Parmenter.

There's probably a Suzie Parmenter in everyone's memory. The perfect teenager. The acne-free adolescent saint who's too goody-goody to like and too cute to hate. At Handley High, Suzie was Head Cheerleader and President of the Student Council. She spent her spare time receiving awards for niceness. Never has anybody smiled so graciously at so many for so long. And just so nobody got the wrong idea about what she meant by those smiles, she developed a permanent shadow named Bubba Stillwell. Bubba played quarterback for Handley High and it was generally agreed that he didn't need a helmet. His skull, like the rest of him, was stronger than steel and twice as thick. At that time, I was ninety-eight pounds of solid muscle, and things that Bubba Stillwell might not like rated some serious thought. So I spent very little time in Suzie's company. A body is a terrible thing to waste.

So I was surprised when she spotted me during intermission. Armed with enough sweetness to put Baby Ruth out of business, she walked right over and *insisted* that I come for dinner on Saturday night. Bubba, still doing his human shadow act, looked down on us and grinned.

How could I refuse? Isn't that every former underdog's dream? Acceptance. Recognition. A triumphant return to the old neighborhood and dinner at Suzie Parmenter Stillwell's house. Of course it never really happens that way, and I know it. But it never dawned on me that it was all a big mistake.

How big? Almost as big as the house that Bubba, now an oil company vice-president, built for Suzie and the kids atop Handley's only hill. By comparison, J.R. Ewing lives in a shack. Only when I got inside, with escape cut off by the maid, two Dobermans and an iron fence, did I realize the magnitude of the error. Somebody had told Suzie that I was the star of a soon-to-premiere ABC situation comedy.

I stood there beneath a life-size replica of that famous Parthenon frieze, "Somebody Slaying Somebody Else," and came up with a really stupid idea: telling the truth. So I explained that I work for one of the many local affiliates of ABC, not the network. My show isn't a comedy—at least not on our better nights. I'm the weatherman on the news in San Diego.

Suzie took it gracefully. But then, she'd probably take World War III gracefully. She and Bubba invited me into their living room, an authentic replica of a sixteenth century baronial hall, where we all sat down and tried not to stare at each other. After about ten minutes of total silence, Bubba thought of something to say.

"Waaahl, ah shore know what you California folks drink," he said, grinning with deceptive innocence.

I followed him to the bar and watched him pour equal parts of Pernod, Tequila and Bubble-Up into his 46-speed blender. The drink, he explained, was called a Worthington Wipe-Out, named after a well-known Los Angeles car dealer. (After one of these, you're ready to trade it in.) Bubba took a hefty sip and survived, so I gave it a try.

As he picked me up off the floor, he explained that this was supposed to be the Official Drink of California. He'd heard about it on a TV talk show. For the first time, I realized why some people hate television.

"We just figgered you'd like it, 'cause ever'body does," Suzie explained as she applied cold compresses to my brow. She checked my pupils, readjusted her Yves St. Laurent cowboy hat, and continued. "It's the latest thing, an' we keep up with the times here in Handley. We got hot tubs an' encounter groups an' women's lib—isn't that right, Bubba?"

Bubba nodded his approval. "She's right, y'know. The li'l person an' me go to non-sexist sensitivity training once a month, an' progressive parenting classes every Thursday, an' ..." He suddenly turned to Suzie in an amazing display of other-centered, non-sexist openness. "Hey, let's take the li'l guy along to our nude self-realization dune buggy races next Saturday!" he said.

Fueled by that Worthington Wipe-Out, my mind conjured a terrible image. Me, nude, at the starting line, revving the engine of a battered VW dune buggy. In the next car, Handley's former gridiron gorilla watched me with something beyond barefaced amusement—and hit the gas on his shiny, supercharged racing machine.

"No thanks," I replied in my best School of Announcing baritone. "Conflicts with my political views." I thought I sounded convincingly cool.

Bubba's face dropped. Then he got another bright idea. "Waaahl, y'kin come to church with us tomorrow, can'tcha?"

At last, an activity that sounded harmless. A bit of "Holy, Holy, Holy" down at good old First Baptist never hurt anybody. So I accepted.

"Yer gonna love it," Bubba said. "We're charter members of the Church of Whatever's Cool. We all git it on tomorrow morning at dawn on a little hill jest outside town."

I worked up the nerve to ask: "In the nude?"

"Oh, good heavens no!" Suzie replied. "Not at a religious ceremony. We all wear robes that don't even have eyeslits. See, it has to be done by feel. You git out yer li'l Hula-Hoop, pull the hood down over yer eyes, an' twirl til yer inner cosmic aura gits in tune with the Rings of Saturn."

I had a chance to think about that the next morning. Rings of Saturn. Nude dune buggy races. In Handley? In the citadel of American virtues? They've even got a franchised chapter of a cult that meets on nights of the full moon to fondle graven images of Leonard Nimoy's ears. And if it's in Handley, it's everywhere. The whole country has become a bunch of imitation California Crazies.

That's the stuff of a serious identity crisis for us authentic California Crazies. Is there nothing that separates us from those followers of fads in Farmington and Fargo? Is there no way we can reassure ourselves that we're still just a bit farther up the tree than anybody else?

As I stood on that hillside at sunrise, draped in a purple robe with no eyeslits, twirling a Hula-Hoop by sense of feel, it came to me. Not the Rings of Saturn, but grunion. Nowhere else in the United States can people fish with their bare hands while standing on the beach. In California, even the fish are crazy.

THESE ARE GRUNION

The Pacific grunion is a small fish native to California's coastal waters. It measures five to eight inches long and about one inch around, giving it the kind of fashionably slender shape you expect in places like Malibu and La Jolla. To complete that "total look," it has a spiffy, two-toned body: blue-green on top, white on the bottom, with a silver racing stripe down each side.

THIS IS NOT A GRUNION

So grunion identification should be no problem. Note the shape and coloring. Then, just to be sure, note the location. If it's in or near the ocean, it's probably a grunion. But don't repeat the mistake made by Louie "Fast Fingers" McGee. On June 22, 1979, Louie saw an object of very similar description parked on Rodeo Drive—alas, right in front of a police car. He explained that he was an amateur ichthyologist, searching for the fabled Giant Grunion. But the judge didn't buy the story. He thought fish should be found in water, and the water in Beverly Hills is toxic to fish. (Only two kinds of water are allowed there: chlorinated and "Bottled in France.") So Louie is now doing time for Grand Theft Auto and Contempt of Court—a tragic consequence of sloppy fish identification. (The stolen Stingray found in Louie's driveway didn't help much, either.)

Fish experts refer to the Pacific grunion as *Leuresthes tenuis*. That figures. The people who gave 'em that name referred to themselves as ichthyologists. Nowadays, fish experts call themselves marine biologists, which certainly is lucky for the rest of us. Keeps us from getting them confused with ichnologists (people who study fossil footprints) and iconologists (people who study symbolic artwork). And brother, that sure avoids a lot of embarassment at cocktail parties.*

There is another kind of grunion: *Leuresthes sardina*, known to their friends as Gulf grunion.

They're slightly longer, skinnier and less colorful, and live in the northern Gulf of California, which is owned by Mexico. Some Arizonans go down there and catch the grunion. But evidently the Mexicans haven't noticed because so far they haven't passed any laws to protect the fish. Maybe they figure there's no profit in seizing sandpails.

This book is mainly about California grunion, which are better known and a whole lot more glamorous. Besides, I can always do a book about Gulf grunion as a sequel, especially if Hollywood buys the movie rights to this one.

*FOOTNOTE: It's also a help to the grunion, who are uneducated and hate big words. Grunion don't even have schools. Some people get that wrong. They figure any fish that likes crowds must have schools. But the grunion is a massing fish, meaning they get together every now and then, but don't hang around together all the time. So if you're cool, you never speak of a "school of grunion," 'cause there is no such thing.

California grunion are a lot like California people. They're individualists who like to follow the crowd. They insist on "doing their own thing," which usually means doing exactly what all their friends are doing. And they especially love big beach parties. Now beach parties may not be particularly radical if you're a person. But for most fish, washing up onto the beach and wiggling around on the sand is about the last thing they'd ever do. The very last thing.

Beach parties are an addiction for the grunion. They get an overwhelming desire for a big bash on the sand about every two weeks during the social season. Like human beach freaks, they usually take up residence within a mile or so of the shore. Then they can slip away from their jobs in the food chain whenever the urge hits 'em.

The similarities between grunion and people really are amazing. Just like us, they all go to the beach at the same times, then gripe about the crowds. Some creatures of the deep—porpoises, for instance—would never be that dumb. But grunion are only human.

Some tourists go slightly bonkers the first time they see hordes of little fishies thronging onto the beach. They've seen movies about the menaces that lurk in the sea!

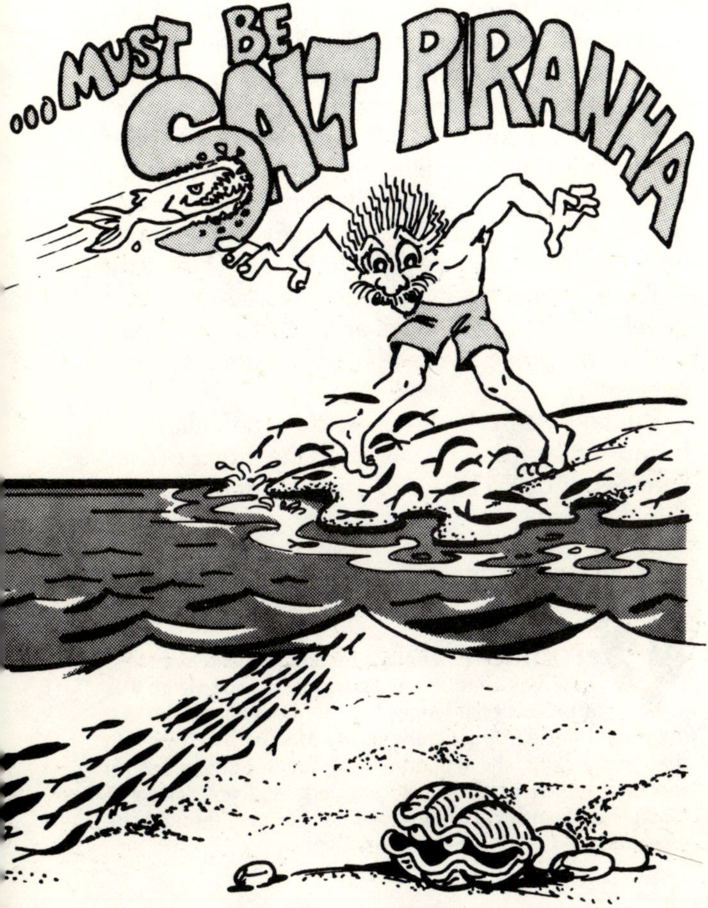
...MUST BE SALT PIRANHA

Their friends back in Iowa warned them about sharks, sting rays, residents of Ocean Beach and other nefarious forms of wildlife. No wonder they're a bit wary.

Then, just when they thought it was safe to go back to the beach, there come the grunion! Zillions of little whatchamacallits in some sort of frenzy, just like a scene from *Attack of the Deadly Birds/Bees/Rats/Bats and/or Name-a-Small-Creature*. You know how those movies go. About ten minutes into the film, the Little Monsters invade. All the sensible people run for cover. But there's always some horn-rimmed ichthyologist who says "Oh, they're quite harmless!" Unaware that they've been eating nuclear wastes and have developed four-inch fangs and a taste for human blood, this yo-yo walks right into the throng and gets eaten.

But take heart. In this case, life can't imitate art because the grunion never go to the movies. Your chances of being killed by grunion are extremely slim.*

*FOOTNOTE: The last recorded fatality was Miss Effie Van Claque, on July 3, 1974. The victim was a professional laugher for TV comedies, who distinguished herself by laughing at *My Mother, The Car*. On that fateful night, she slipped while grunion hunting, fell on top of a bunch of slimy little wigglers, and got tickled to death. Her friends could've saved her but they thought she was practicing.

SAN ONOFRE
SEND ME ANOTHER ICHTHYOLOGIST.
THEY'RE DELICIOUS!

However, most tourists and a lot of natives have never even seen a grunion. They think grunion hunting is like snipe hunting: the unthinking, guided by the unfeeling, in pursuit of the nonexistent. But they're wrong.

There really are grunion. And they really do go to the beach. They just keep different hours.

People have to go on hot summer afternoons when they can use their sunhats, sunglasses and tanning lotions. Grunion can't afford those things, even on sale. So they go at night—a very good idea, since it keeps them away from people who just bought a lot of expensive sun gear and wouldn't mind saving a few bucks on dinner.

But just any night won't do. Mother Nature orders her grunion ashore only at certain times: about every two weeks, one to four nights after the two highest tides of the month, roughly thirty minutes after the high tide of the day, March through August only. On the Pacific coast, those tides always fall at night.*

So the grunion are on the beach with the almost-highest tide-caused waves of the month, and at no other times. Unlike people, grunion never try to beat the system, and they are almost impossible to fool. You'll never see grunion on the beach in October, no matter how good the weather. They don't come in at low tide, even if a storm makes the waves unusually high. They don't forget which day it is, even if clouds block out the moon, or if heavy rains change the salt content of the water. So far, even pollution doesn't seem to foul up the grunion's sense of timing, though it certainly seems to foul up almost everything else.

We don't know how the grunion always sense when it's time for a beach bash, but they do. A couple of days in advance, they start to gather offshore, to wait for the appointed hour. When it comes, even earthquakes can't distract them. Marine biologists have yet to figure out how a fish which otherwise shows no special intellectual gifts can manage such a high level of concentration.

They should ask the teenagers, who go to about the same places at roughly the same times, for very similar purposes. Teenagers, too, show sudden flashes of genius which aren't used at other times—like during school. I remember an extreme case, back at Handley High. Jimmy-Joe Fogg memorized the names, addresses, class schedules and approximate measurements of 257 different girls—yet flunked history because he couldn't remember when the War of 1812 was fought. Such mystifying behavior could only be instinctive.

*FOOTNOTE: Gulf grunion have a different schedule from Pacific grunion. Their season runs February through May. And because of the Gulf of California's long, narrow shape, tides there may be very different from tides on the Pacific coast, a comparatively short distance away. So in the Gulf, grunion tides often occur during the day.

But which instinct?

We can rule out clothing and shelter. Grunion don't need 'em. And since they aren't fond of cheeseburgers, they couldn't be coming for the food. So—you guessed it—the grunion come to "spawn."

This is a family book, so I won't translate that into teenager terms. But if you have any doubts, they can be easily erased by reading the inscriptions (which can't be erased) on walls, rocks and T-shirts found near the beach.

Teenagers may get their kicks from writing about it. But grunion don't. Thank Heavens! Grunion are famous for their scandalous behavior. They spawn in large groups, the more the merrier, and don't give a darn what people think. With such shocking lack of decorum, there's no telling what grunion would write if they ever got their hot little fins on a can of spray paint!

33

Someone had to invent a more proper phrase for what grunion do. And that task fell to Jbmrzy Zgnrsky, a former Washington powermonger and part-time political prophet. Jbmrz, as he's known to his remaining friends, almost came to power by almost coining the slogan for the Goldwater campaign. His version was "A choice! Not a chance!" The last half of that was changed from "Not a chance!" to "Not an echo." And though thinkers like Jbmrz don't exactly grow on trees, his cronies never quite forgave him for getting it right the first time.

So Jbmrz moved to California and rented a beach house. He loved to go out at night and meditate, sitting in the waves as the tide came in. It comforted him to know that other things got washed up, too. One night, while contemplating Jerry Brown's presidential chances, he looked down and found himself surrounded by fish. Zillions of little fish, all hurrying to get out of the water. He searched his mind, trying to imagine the reason. Then it dawned on him. If people-candidates tested the water, fish candidates probably tested the land. The fish had to be running. But for what? He picked one up and asked him where he stood on the issues. The little fellow had absolutely nothing to say. Jbmrz felt that old lust for power coursing through his veins again. Here, at last, was the perfect candidate: energetic, yet cool, and incapable of putting his foot in his mouth. Jbmrz offered to coin a slogan for the fish. But as he stood up, he found that he was also surrounded by Treasury Agents. They wanted to ask him about some of the phrases he'd been coining in the cellar—like "In God We Trust" and "Federal Reserve Note."

So Jbmrz never did get proper credit for coining the phrase "grunion run." But he did get a chance to use his talents again, coining phrases on personalized license plates.

Maybe it's just as well. Jbmrz had an uncanny knack for getting the words right and the meanings wrong. Grunion don't run the way candidates run. It's more like the way runners run. In fact, you could think of a grunion run as a sort of fishy Boston Marathon. The similarities are remarkable. Thousands of beady-eyed fanatics gather in one place. Somebody says "go" and they all rush off in the same direction, all wearing the same do-or-die expression.

I guess that's why I can't look at a grunion run without thinking about Uncle Titus, who took up running at the age of 74. He'd get up at 5:00 a.m. and run for one solid hour. Then he'd spend the rest of his waking hours talking about it and applying poultices to his knees. Grunion have an advantage over Uncle Titus. No knees.

We pretty much know why grunion run. But people are another matter. I once asked a lady jogger why she ran, and spent the next two hours listening to a detailed explanation of my miserable physical condition, my bad habits and my imminent physical collapse. It was about as much fun as listening to a professional nonsmoker.

Anyway, people who run are pursuing good muscle tone, cardiovascular fitness and/or mental health (by getting out of the house for an hour). Grunion run for entirely different reasons. They're pursuing other grunion and don't care about improving their lungs, since they don't have any.

But they do work out between runs. They stick to a year-around fitness and conditioning schedule. Every day they go out and get lots of exercise by swimming as fast as they can. They never smoke, probably because their itsy-bitsy Bics don't flick underwater. And they never drink alcohol. Adult grunion stick to a high-protein diet consisting of any small-but-not-too-agile fish they meet.* It's an inspired program of clean living and natural food—inspired, that is, by bigger fish who regard the grunion as healthful, natural food.

---

*FOOTNOTE: What different kinds of fish eat isn't just a matter of taste. It's largely a methodology problem. Some fish strain microscopic plants and animals from the water as they swim. Others operate by sense of smell, or even by touch. But adult grunion fall into the "sight feeders" category. Like many other fish, they keep their eyes open. Dinner time is any time they spot a fish that's smaller and slower than they are.

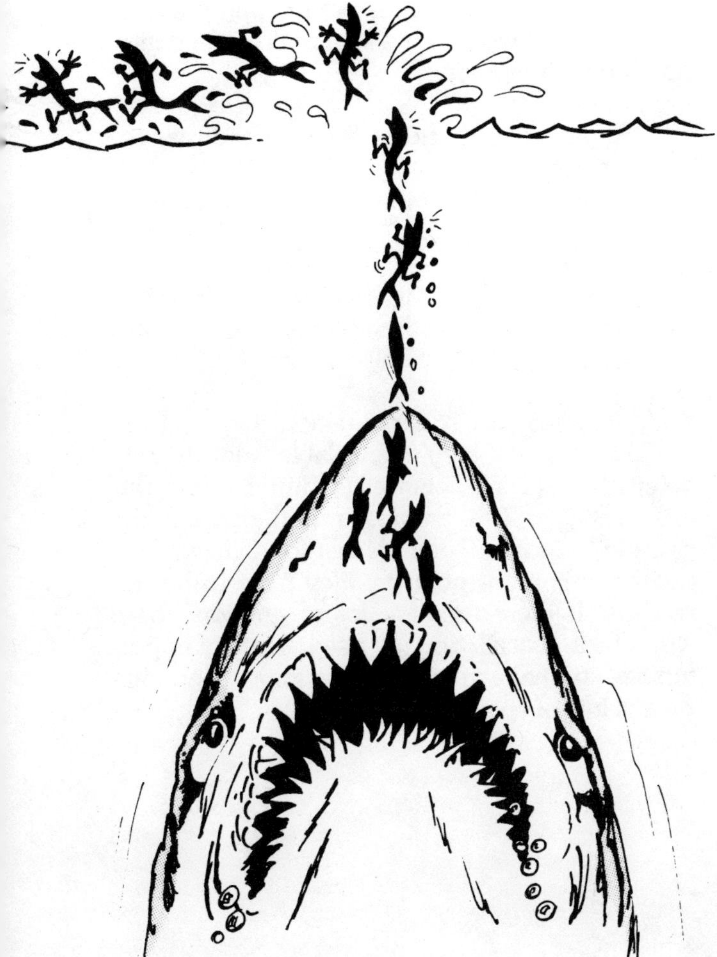

It's a fish-eat-fish world out there. But hungry fish aren't the grunion's only problem.

Almost everything else eats grunion, too. Birds. People. Dogs and cats. Plus fish too numerous to mention—so I won't. It's a lot easier to list things that don't eat grunion.

1. Anything that's not around. (For instance, penguins which live in Antarctica.)
2. Anything that's not hungry at the moment.
3. Strict vegetarians.
4. Very small critters.
5. Picky eaters. (Some species have diets limited to specific other species. Also, some kids eat only chicken-salad sandwiches.)

It's definitely a circular situation. Grunion are popular because they're available and virtually defenseless. (Their defense is swimming fast. But lots of bigger fish are faster and outrank the grunion in Mother Nature's fast-food chain.) Because grunion are popular, they have to be numerous. If there aren't a lot of grunion, there won't be any at all. So they need plenty of opportunities to make more little grunion. And that means lots of spawning runs.

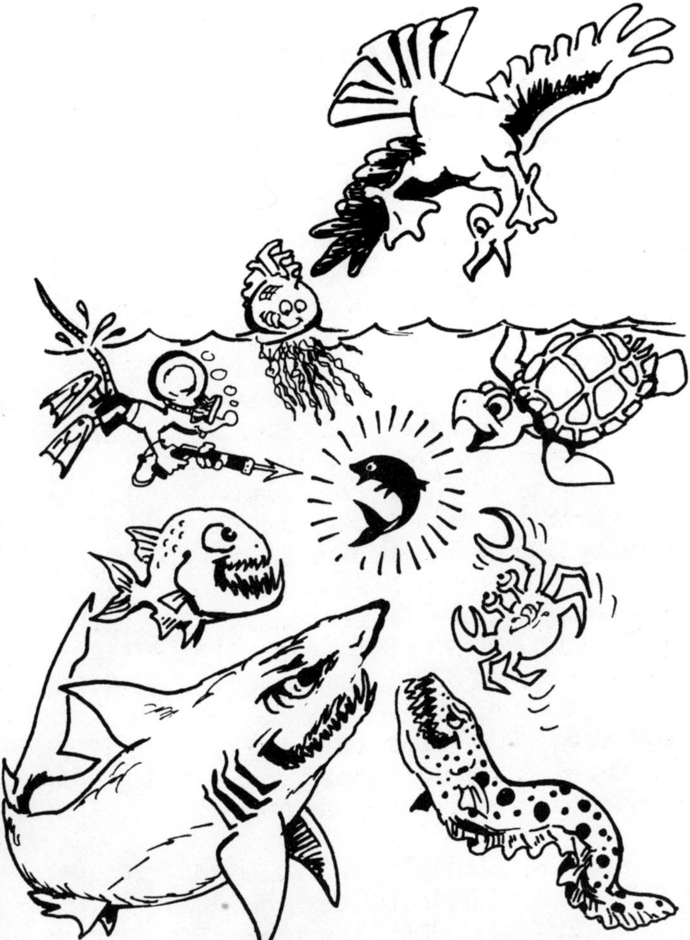

Grunion Run Predictions

San Diego and Los Angeles

1981

Wed.	March 11	1:01AM	Thu.	June 4	10:57PM
Thu.	March 12	2:05AM	Fri.	June 5	11:46PM
Fri.	March 13	3:27AM	Sun.	June 7	12:41AM
Sat.	March 21	10:28PM	Thu.	June 18	9:49PM
Sun.	March 22	10:49PM	Fri.	June 19	10:21PM
Mon.	March 23	11:15PM	Sat.	June 20	10:57PM
Thu.	April 9	12:27AM	Fri.	July 3	10:42PM
Fri.	April 10	1:33AM	Sat.	July 4	11:27PM
Sat.	April 11	2:55AM	Mon.	July 6	12:12AM
Tue.	April 21	10:34PM	Fri.	July 17	9:37PM
Wed.	April 22	11:00PM	Sat.	July 18	10:12PM
Thu.	April 23	11:32PM	Sun.	July 19	10:51PM
Wed.	May 6	11:13PM	Fri.	July 31	9:47PM
Fri.	May 8	12:04AM	Sat.	August 1	10:26PM
Sat.	May 9	1:07AM	Sun.	August 2	11:05PM
Wed.	May 20	10:05PM	Mon.	August 17	10:42PM
Thu.	May 21	10:34PM	Tue.	August 18	11:27PM
Fri.	May 22	11:09PM	Thu.	August 20	12:22AM

Remember, all dates in April and May are closed to fishing. But grunion watchers are always welcome.

Grunion Run Predictions
San Diego and Los Angeles

1982

Fri	March 12	11:34PM	Mon.	June 7	9:44PM
Sun.	March 14	12:04AM	Tue.	June 8	10:13PM
			Wed.	June 9	10:42PM
Tue.	March 30	12:38AM	Wed.	June 23	11:00PM
Wed.	March 31	1:42AM	Thu.	June 24	11:52PM
Thu.	April 1	3:09AM	Sat.	June 26	12:51AM
Sat.	April 10	10:45PM	Wed.	July 7	9:58PM
Sun.	April 11	11:11PM	Thu.	July 8	10:33PM
Mon.	April 12	11:37PM	Fri.	July 9	11:08PM
Wed.	April 28	12:17AM	Thu.	July 22	10:50PM
Thu.	April 29	1:24AM	Fri.	July 23	11:38PM
Fri.	April 30	2:53AM	Sun.	July 25	12:27AM
Sun.	May 9	10:07PM	Fri.	August 6	10:18PM
Mon.	May 10	10:34PM	Sat.	August 7	10:52PM
Tue.	May 11	11:03PM	Sun.	August 8	11:34PM
Tue.	May 25	11:11PM	Fri.	August 20	10:34PM
Thu.	May 27	12:03AM	Sat.	August 21	11:20PM
Fri.	May 28	1:12AM	Mon.	August 23	12:06AM

Remember, all dates in April and May are closed to fishing. But grunion watchers are always welcome.

Grunion Run Predictions

San Diego and Los Angeles

1983

Sun.	March 20	12:41AM	Mon.	June 13	11:07PM
Mon.	March 21	1:42AM	Wed.	June 15	12:03AM
Tue.	March 22	3:13AM	Thu.	June 16	1:09AM
Thu.	March 31	11:24PM	Sun.	June 26	9:55PM
Sat.	April 2	Midnight	Mon.	June 27	10:30PM
Sun.	April 3	12:35AM	Tue.	June 28	11:02PM
Sat.	April 16	11:24PM	Tue.	July 12	11:02PM
Mon.	April 18	12:14AM	Wed.	July 13	11:56PM
Tue.	April 19	1:20AM	Fri.	July 15	12:53AM
Fri.	April 29	10:44PM	Mon.	July 25	9:43PM
Sat.	April 30	11:13PM	Tue.	July 26	10:15PM
Sun.	May 1	11:45PM	Wed.	July 27	10:47PM
Sun.	May 15	11:11PM	Wed.	August 10	10:53PM
Tue.	May 17	12:08AM	Thu.	August 11	11:42PM
Wed.	May 18	1:17AM	Sat.	August 13	12:41AM
Fri.	May 27	9:43PM	Wed.	August 24	9:59PM
Sat.	May 28	10:14PM	Thu.	August 25	10:28PM
Sun.	May 29	10:46PM	Fri.	August 26	11:03PM

Remember, all dates in April and May are closed to fishing. But grunion watchers are always welcome.

The Catch to Catching Grunion

As everyone knows, tides are caused by the moon. Its gravity pulls on the water, causing two bulges—one on the side of the earth that's closest, the other on the opposite side.

But the moon's gravity isn't the only force pulling on the oceans. The sun's gravity, powerful enough to keep the whole planet in its orbit, is also at work. Because of the sun's vastly greater distance from earth, its pull isn't as obvious as the moon's. But it's there, and it is very strong. The proof of that occurs twice a month, when the sun and moon fall into a pulling line. Their effects combine and cause the much-higher *spring tides*. That term refers to the way the tides seem to "spring" up, not to the season. But spring tides that occur during the spring and summer months are followed in one or two days by grunion tides.

You'd think we could predict grunion runs for the next century, at least. But we can't. The astronomical data is the easy, reliable part. Unfortunately, a few dozen not-so-easy factors affect the tides, too.

Like what? Like the shape of the coastline, its distance from other coastlines, the depth of the water, the sizes and shapes of underwater mountains, volcanic activity that changes the ocean floor and, of course, earthquakes. And those are just for starters.

So our 1982 and 1983 predictions, formulated in late 1980, could be off by the time you need them. That's the bad news. The good news is that if there are any changes, they'll be reflected in the times the TV weatherman reads.

But back to the bad news now. Beside tides, there are a lot of fishy details that can come between you and your midnight snack.

When the TV weatherman announces that the grunion will run at 11:47 tonight, he really means that *some* grunion will run on *some* beaches between 11:47 p.m. and about 2:00 a.m.—or maybe even 2:30 a.m. Time is tight in the TV business, so he probably won't mention that some grunion will wait til tomorrow night, and some may even wait til the night after that, and some beaches won't see any action at all this month. Nobody knows which beaches the grunion will use on any given night, especially TV weathermen, who aren't generally held in very high regard by the grunion.

Picking the wrong beach used to be a minor problem. If the time arrived and the grunion didn't, you could just load the gang back into the car and drive to another beach.

Since grunion runs can last for more than an hour, you had a fair chance of getting your hot little hands on a few cold little fish before the night was done.

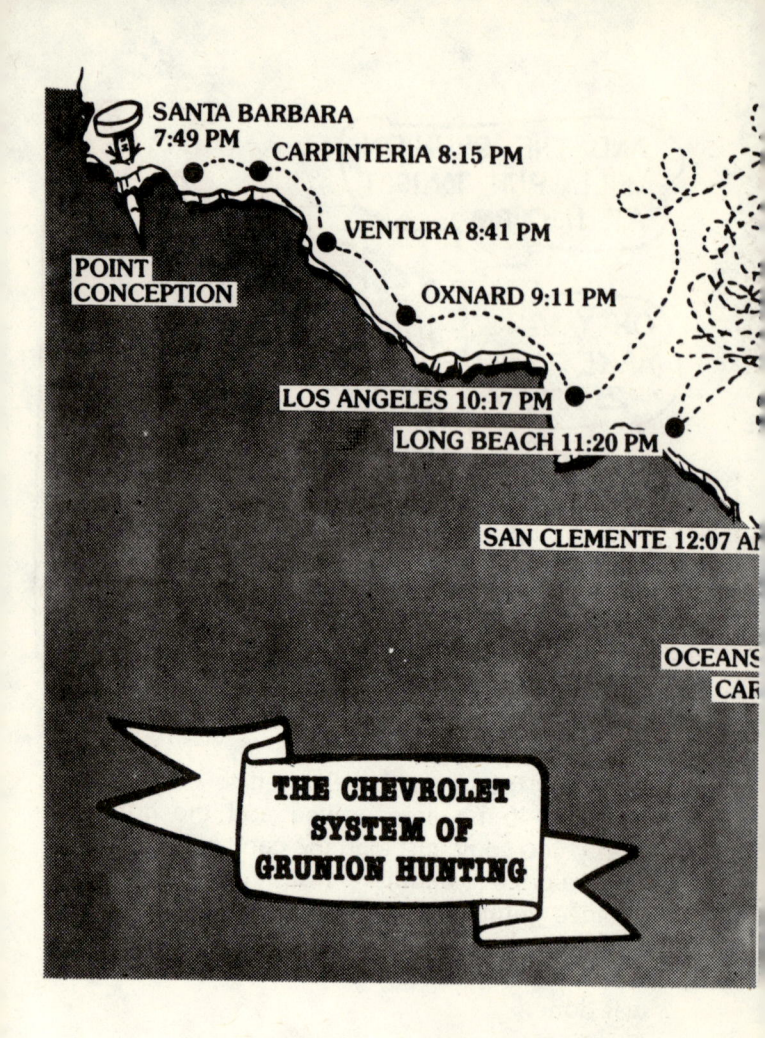

SANTA BARBARA 7:49 PM
CARPINTERIA 8:15 PM
VENTURA 8:41 PM
POINT CONCEPTION
OXNARD 9:11 PM
LOS ANGELES 10:17 PM
LONG BEACH 11:20 PM
SAN CLEMENTE 12:07 A
OCEANS
CAR

THE CHEVROLET SYSTEM OF GRUNION HUNTING

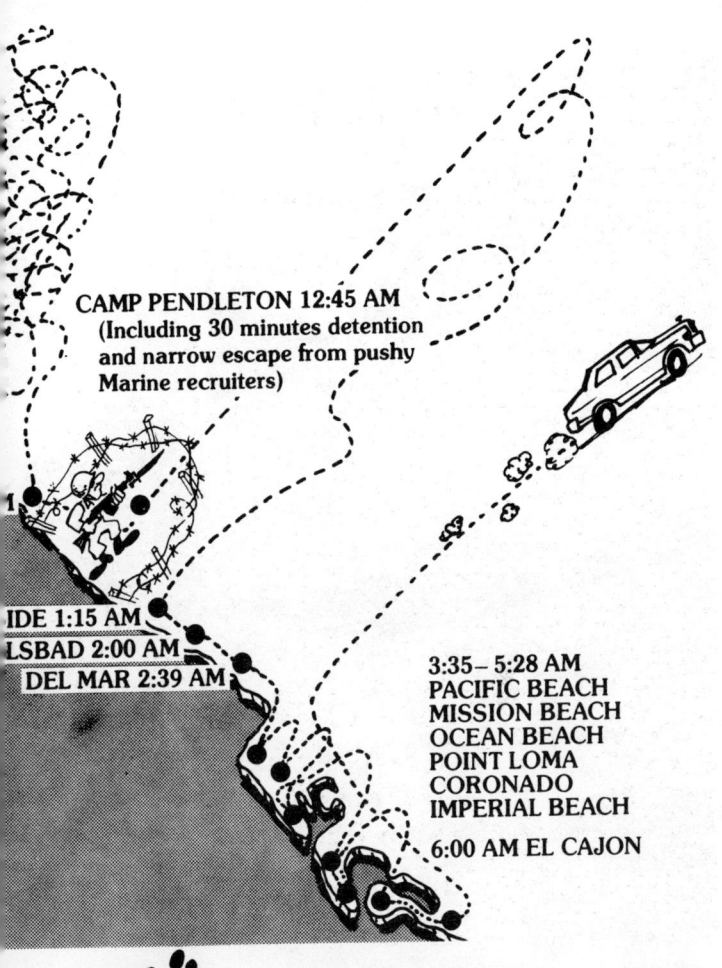

CAMP PENDLETON 12:45 AM
(Including 30 minutes detention
and narrow escape from pushy
Marine recruiters)

IDE 1:15 AM
LSBAD 2:00 AM
DEL MAR 2:39 AM

3:35 – 5:28 AM
PACIFIC BEACH
MISSION BEACH
OCEAN BEACH
POINT LOMA
CORONADO
IMPERIAL BEACH

6:00 AM EL CAJON

*FOOTNOTE: If we'd been smart, we would've started in the south and moved progressively northward, since that's what the tides do. The high tides don't occur at exactly the same instant all along the Pacific Coast. They arrive just a bit earlier in the south, later in the north.

Unfortunately, at today's gas prices, The Chevrolet System of Grunion Hunting has become very expensive. Last time I tried it, my plate of grunion cost $68.50,* wine and vegetables not included.

*FOOTNOTE: For the same money, you can have lobster with vintage wine and all the trimmings, served by a waiter in a tux, at your favorite fine restaurant. As a matter of taste, the author finds that a lot more appealing than pan-fried grunion, laced with sand and washed down with Fed-Mart chablis.

A grunionless grunion hunt can happen to anyone. For those embarrassing moments, it's best to have a few of the classic fishermen's excuses memorized. "I threw the small ones back" works very well, especially since all grunion are small. "I just went along to help the kids" is good too, unless you happen to be a bachelor like me. But that angler's standby, "I should've brought heavier tackle" tends to draw more smirks than sympathy. What did you need? An elephant gun?

It's legal to catch grunion when they come to the beach to spawn. But there are rules.
1. You must have a California fishing license if you're over 16 years of age.
2. You must catch them only with your bare hands. No traps or nets allowed.
3. No grunion hunting during April or May. Those runs are set aside to allow the fish to reproduce and insure their survival.
4. The state doesn't set a limit on the number you can catch, as long as you play by the rules. But you really shouldn't catch more than you can eat.

Wardens from the Department of Fish and Game do patrol the beaches on grunion nights, and a salt water fishing license costs only $5. (It's available at most sporting goods stores.) Since illegal grunion grabbing is a misdemeanor punishable by a $500 fine or six months in the slammer, it might be a good idea to get yourself a license.

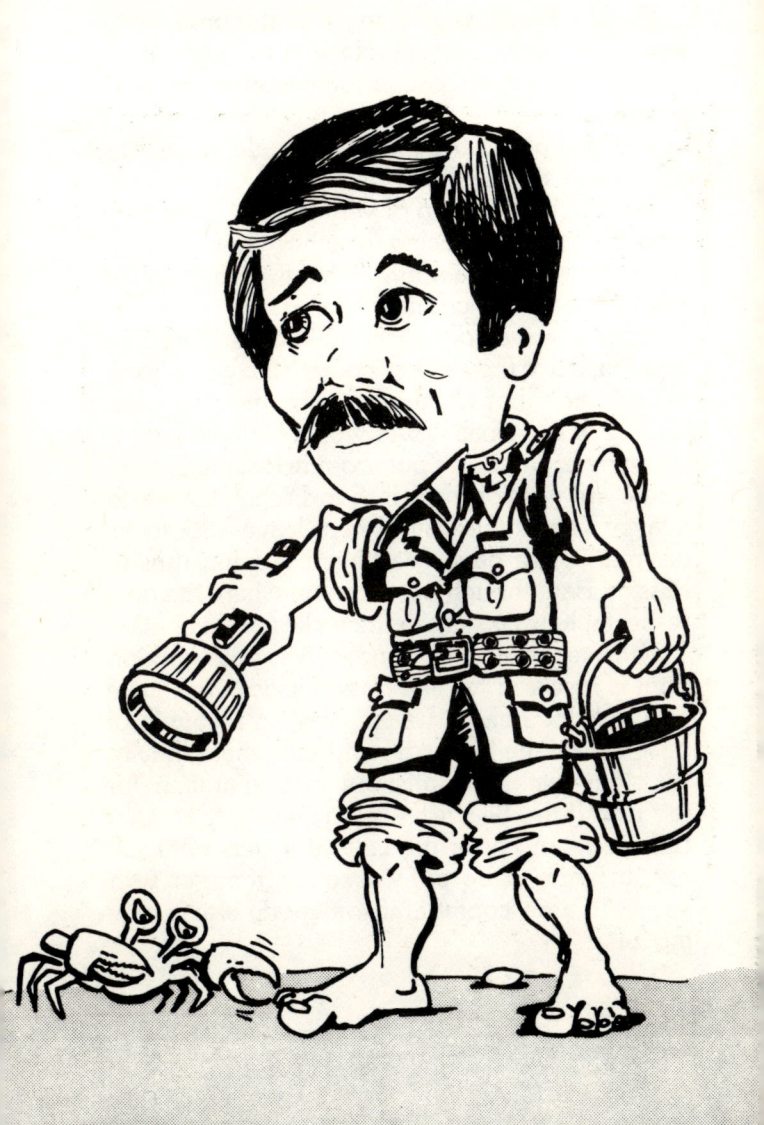

There are two ways to increase the probability that you'll be in the right place at the right time. The first is to choose a beach with grunion appeal.

Grunion prefer beaches with moderate slopes at or near the high-tide line. They don't like a beach that's very steep or very shallow. And they tend to like west-facing beaches best—except when they choose a north- or south-facing beach, just to one-up the grunion hunters.

Regular waves of moderate size also help the grunion, since they sort of bodysurf to get ashore. So a beach that always has crummy, irregular, too-big or too-small waves would have less grunion appeal. But don't put too much stake in that. There are grunion runs in San Diego Bay—and heaven knows the waves there leave a lot to be desired. There have even been grunion runs in Mission Bay (though not recently) where the only respectable waves are in the wakes of ski boats.

The second way to insure a first-class grunion hunt is reserved for first-class fanatics. You have to watch the coastal waters, starting a couple of days before the high tide, and see where they're massing—gathering offshore in preparation for the run. If the beach has a conveniently located cliff, you can check the coastal waters easily. If not, it helps to be a TV weather reporter with access to a helicopter that somebody else is paying for.

Look for a fairly large, dark blob in the water, several hundred yards offshore. That'll be the grunion—unless it turns out to be anchovies* or just one of the general-purpose dark blobs that occur in the ocean, here and there.

But if it is the grunion, you can be sure they'll run on the closest beach on one of the nights listed on the schedule, at roughly the specified time. Probably.

Every so often, grunion will mass near a beach and not run. Nobody knows why. The only thing that's sure is that they don't mass near one beach, then swim away and spawn on another. That's just not the way grunion operate.

So although there are things you can do to improve your chances of being around when the grunion are, you'll never bat a thousand. Only one person *ever* did that.

---

*FOOTNOTE: There is a way to tell anchovies from massed grunion without rowing out for a closer look. Anchovies are a "school" fish. They *stream*, moving from place to place. A school of anchovies, seen from above, should be longer and thinner and headed somewhere. Grunion, on the other hand, should just sit there. Their pattern will be the classic "blob" shape.

Holly Golly is one of those people you meet if you appear on television. Now don't get me wrong. I have nothing against those who march to a different drummer, in a different direction, in a different uniform. Except they always seem to want marching companions and have me in mind for the job.

She came by to see me at work one afternoon: just an ordinary, green-haired girl with a large, black bird sitting on her shoulder. She told me The Spirits were being naughty again. They planned to have a good laugh on everybody by turning on all the faucets at 11:56 p.m.

Well I'd seen the weather service data. It was a fair and warmer situation, pure and simple. So I handled the matter with my usual professional smoothness: I thanked her for the information and hid in the closet until she'd left the building.

At 11:56 p.m., I was driving home after the Late News. And sure enough, drops started hitting my windshield. I didn't let it bother me. I'd been outguessed by some ding-a-ling who was wearing her headband too tight. Big deal. My Aunt Greta predicts rain, too. That's arthritis, not The Supernatural.

A few days later, I received a letter, postmarked Portland. It was from Holly. She said she was going to be away from San Diego for quite some time, helping Uncle Sven. (*Sven-Golly!!*) He had a hot project brewing on a nearby mountain. So she wanted me to have her personal copy of The Official Grunion Schedule—the same one The Spirits gave to the grunion.

It was written in small print on a squashed piece of kelp: beach by beach, the exact times the grunion would arrive. The runs I checked out were accurate to the minute. It began to dawn on me that Holly wasn't your average kook. She was a kook with *connections!*

It made a lot of difference in my attitude. I tried to get ahold of her by letter, then by phone. Finally, I caught a plane to Seattle. Her apartment above the Blood Bank was vacant. But a doctor who worked the night shift downstairs (and spoke with an odd European accent) said Holly and Uncle Sven were at a cookout. I put two and two together. *Mountain. Cookout. Hot project. Sven-Golly!* It may be years before anyone breaks my record for getting to the airport, fast.

Two days later, Mount St. Helens blew. I know Holly and her Uncle are all right. I know they're somewhere—preferably a long way away. It's not that I don't want to know exactly when and where the grunion will run. But some things just aren't worth it.

Lacking Holly's inside information about grunion behavior, most people just trust to luck. Crossing your fingers isn't going to make it any easier to hold onto a grunion. You can try a lucky charm. But those things never work for me. I keep losing them. And a penny in the shoe isn't a good choice, either. Shoes are expensive these days, and I have yet to see one that looked any better for being soaked in salt water and caked with sand. As for rabbits' feet—show me one that came off a lucky rabbit.

So when superstition fails, mankind traditionally turns to science. But for us grunion hunters, that's not much help, either. Scientists may be making great strides toward solving nature's mysteries. However, some mysteries pay better than others. Grunion behavior is definitely one of the "others."

I don't mean to give the impression that nobody is studying these loveable fish. A small but dedicated group of untrained amateurs, mostly under the age of twelve, is giving it their best. Maybe their research hasn't yielded much. But what can you expect from someone who works for 50 cents an hour or less. And some of their discoveries should be very interesting—to those who'll try anything once.

Grunionology Discovery No. 1
Grunion Calling

This was the first major breakthrough by Rodney S. Bratanowsky, a genius I'm sure we'll hear from again, though perhaps not for a while. Amazingly, he was only ten years old when he began working on his Theory of Stereo Attraction. (He's now eleven.)

He started by studying bird calls, then hog calls, and worked his way up to snake charming—until his mom found the snake. Then there was nothing to do but go ahead with The Big Experiment.

He recorded the sounds of spawning female grunion,* using the best equipment available: his dad's stereo system. Two weeks later, he returned to the same beach, put the apparatus in the water and turned it on. It worked perfectly—for about five seconds. Then it quit, never to be heard from again. But the experiment was a success. The grunion showed up on the beach a few minutes later. Unfortunately, so did Rodney's dad.

Rodney still has a lot of research to do, to prove that the grunion came in response to the sound, and not by coincidence. And some day he may get his chance. But lately, he's much too busy mowing lawns, washing cars and baby-sitting. It isn't easy for a kid his age to earn $957.50 for a new stereo system.

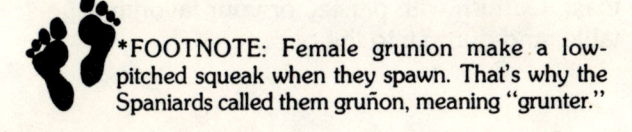

*FOOTNOTE: Female grunion make a low-pitched squeak when they spawn. That's why the Spaniards called them gruñon, meaning "grunter."

Grunionology Discovery No. 2
Grunion Bait

This works on the same principle as the Flyby-nite Trout Attractant you've seen advertised in magazines like *Backwoods Mechanic* and *Popular Gunman*. And it carries the same guarantee—which applies only during odd-numbered leap years. So for what it's worth ($4.98 plus shipping and handling), here's the recipe:

2 Fresh Brontosaurus Eggs
3 cups Sliced Roadapples
½ keg Recycled Downstream Beer
1 can Campbell's Cream of
   Mushroom Soup

Simmer, uncovered, in a two-quart saucepan, for three minutes. Serve over a bed of rice or melba toast. Garnish with parsley or your favorite vegetable, and dump into the ocean.

Grunionology Discovery No. 3
Grunion Dancing

Only a natural-born dancer could've made this amazing discovery. And that's what Lulu Goodbody was. She started life kicking and wiggling, and never stopped. She could've grown up to be a female Rudolf Nureyev, if only she'd had the training. Everyone who knew her agreed she rarely had both feet on the ground.

But Lulu's family was too poor for ballet lessons. Her daddy was a hat salesman and the fedora business was way down. So sometimes her parents took her to the beach on grunion nights. It was a surefire way to pick up an extra buck. Lulu did her rendition of "Tea for Two" and her dad passed one of his unsold hats. They could've made big money if she'd had a chance to do her encore. But the grunion always came to the beach after her first number and took the crowds away. Her dad figured it was just bad luck.

Lulu dropped out of school at the age of sixteen. (It was for the best. Algebra is next to impossible when you spend that much time twirling.) She couldn't find a job. But her social life was a different matter. Overnight, Lulu became the hit of the Ocean Beach party circuit. No bash was complete without her version of *Swan Lake,* performed on the coffee table. Unfortunately, fads change fast in O.B. And before the year was out, so was Lulu.

That didn't stop her, though. If she couldn't dance on tables at parties, she'd just find another place. The Ocean Beach jetty seemed ideal, and she certainly liked the fresh air better than that funny-smelling smoke that tends to accumulate in Ocean Beach apartments.

Soon word got out. Dance buffs, mostly from fraternities at San Diego State, started hanging around the jetty, hoping for a chance to see Lulu strut her stuff. Soon, others joined them: TV weathermen, Navy recruits and large numbers of amateur photographers. Everyone wanted to see "The Jetty Dancer," especially the cops.

What a predicament! At last, she had her chance at fame and fortune, guest shots on talk shows and maybe even a lounge act in Vegas. Her big break—and she didn't have a thing to wear! Lulu's tutu was long gone and she didn't have the money to buy another.

Then she remembered the dance she'd done as a child and got an idea. She enlisted a few dozen fraternity pledges and went to the beach on the next grunion night.

She opened with "Tea for Two" and the grunion came in on the next wave. Then, just as she'd planned, the audience kept watching and the pledges went after the fish. (Well, some of 'em did.) When the run was over, Lulu's friends were the only ones who had any grunion. They raised $435.50 selling take-home fish after the show.

Lulu got her costume, a full-length ballet gown, and returned to the jetty. This time, however, nobody seemed interested. Her chance at stardom had flown. But one good looking ichthyology student was still hanging around. She married him and took a job teaching aerobic dance.

As for her method of bringing grunion to the beach, it might work for you, too—provided you look like Lulu, move like Lulu and, especially dress like Lulu. It's an idea several scholars I know would like to study further. Much further.

But just when you figure there's no chance of seeing a grunion anywhere in the neighborhood, a few stalwart little males will flip themselves out of the next wave and wiggle around on the sand.

Don't catch 'em! They're scouts, come to test the sand and check out the grunion hunter situation. Traditionally, good grunion hunters switch off their flashlights and their mouths, so the scouts will return with a good report.

And what if somebody does catch the scouts? Well, the grunion might run anyway. You see, there's another theory which explains the fact that a grunion run is always preceded by a few males who flop onto the sand, then return with the next wave. They could be plain ordinary gun-jumpers.

According to the gun-jumper theory, the grunion are massed offshore, ready to go, like runners ready to start a race. And a couple of them always get a bit too revved up. Most of the grunion are still out there, building up steam and waiting for the right moment. And it won't be long before they decide it's time. But there are always a few in every crowd who just get a bit too itchy.

When the gang finally decides to go, they catch the next wave (and the next, and the next), and sort of surf onto the beach. The females high-tail it to the high tide line and wiggle their back ends into the sand, til they're up to their shapely little pectoral fins. The males—maybe half a dozen of them—snuggle as close as they can. The female wiggles back and forth, depositing her eggs, while the males release their milt, which will filter down to fertilize them. Then the guys split.* The female must wiggle her way out of the sand alone. Any helping hand will come from a grunion hunter, not her fly-by-night boyfriends.

That brings us to a difficult dilemma: good grunion hunting versus good conservation. The fish are here and gone in a minute or so, and the biggest are always females. So if you grab first and ask questions later, you'll take mostly females—and eliminate a lot of future grunion. A female can spawn four to eight times a year. Depending on her age, she'll produce two or three thousand eggs each time. So a good conservationist takes only males—and settles for a smaller dinner. But even if you want big, meaty females in your frying pan, you can at least wait until she's finished spawning.

*FOOTNOTE: When a female has finished spawning, she's through til the next run. But that's not necessarily so for the guys. On their way back, they just might see another female headed for the beach and . . . Anyhow, that may be why males seem to outnumber females by three or four to one.

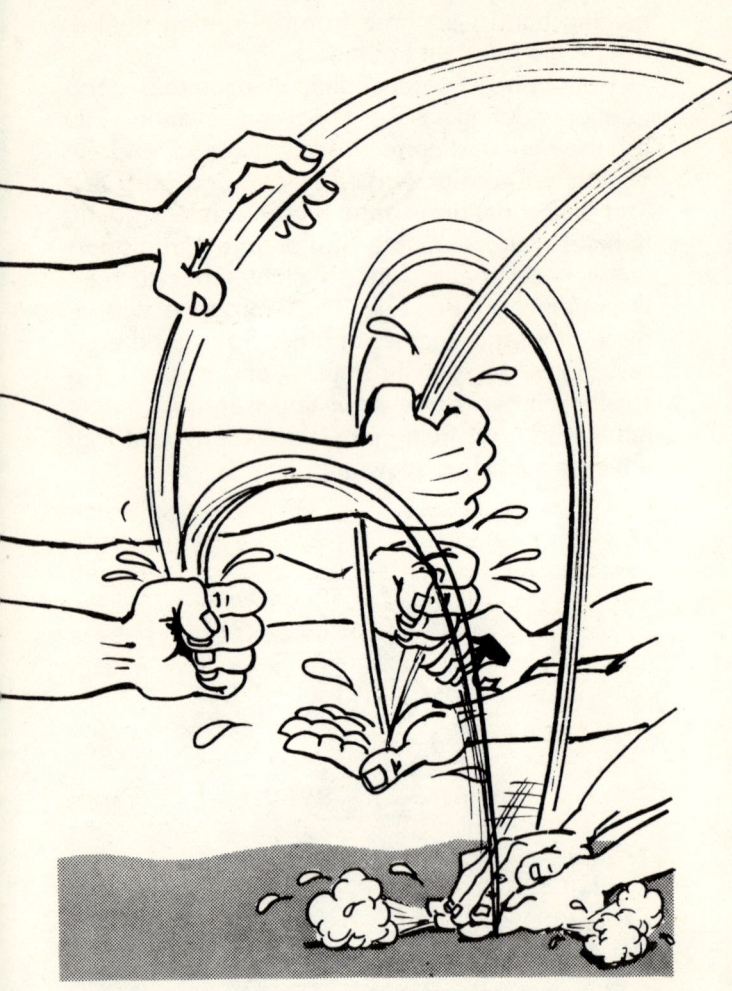

Whichever grunion you grab for, it won't be as easy as it sounds. Grunion are about as easy to hold on to as a gyrating bar of wet soap. They have special glands in their skins which secrete a slippery substance. That protects them against parasite infections when they're in the water, and against grunion hunters when they're out of the water. Trout fishermen may tell their tales about "the one that got away." But with grunion hunters, it's never just one.

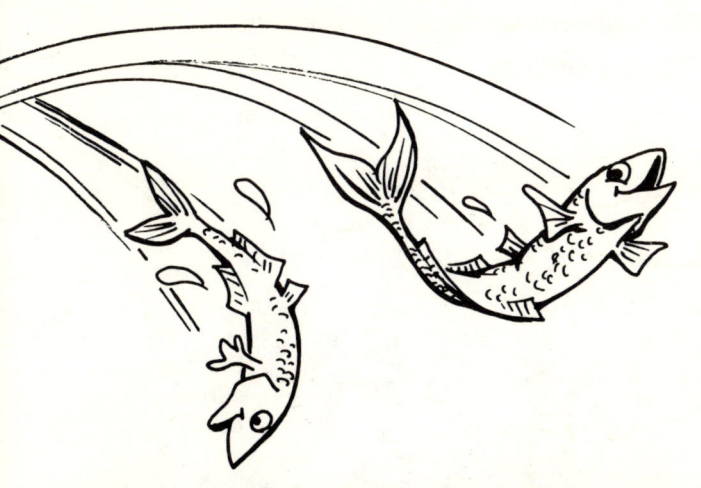

Grunion skins are durable, as well as slippery. They have to be. The sand they spawn in is very abrasive stuff. So although some type of fish are too delicate to survive if they're taken, then thrown back, grunion will usually do just fine. Of course, if it's been beating itself silly in your sandpail for the last five minutes, it may be too far gone. But apart from that, if you don't want grunion for dinner, but do want a closer look, you can pick the fish up, inspect it, and slip it back into the wave with reasonable certainty that it's no worse for the wear.

So now a few words about equipment:
Don't overdo it!

Pail for carrying fish

Flashlight to look at grunion

Friend to help kill time while waiting

Bellybutton
(Don't leave
home without it!)
Pockets
(optional)
Vented shoes

Note that the ideal grunion hunter is under twelve years of age. There are six major reasons why kids make the best grunion hunters:

1. They're closer to the ground.
2. They love to run around until they're totally exhausted.
3. They don't mind getting cold, wet and covered with sand.
4. They keep their minds on grunion hunting, and aren't inhibited by worries about what all the seawater, sand and smelly goop they collect might do to the car's interior.
5. They don't stop at just a few fish, figuring that the more they catch, the more they'll have to clean and cook. After all, what are mommies and daddies for?
6. They don't even need fishing licenses.

So if you've got kids, you're set. If you don't, you may find that friends and relatives are surprisingly willing to lend theirs out for a grunion hunt, usually suggesting that you not return them too quickly.

When you get to the beach, you'll have some time to kill. If you've brought the required number of pint-sized cyclones, you have two alternatives. You can let them do what comes naturally—picking fights, screaming and harassing the adults. Or you can find a constructive activity.

Organizing a team and running a few drills keeps the kids in line and lets you indulge a favorite fantasy: that of being a better strategist than those dudes who lucked out and ended up with whole NFL teams to mastermind. And the best part is, you can't go wrong. There's no such thing as bad grunion-hunting strategy because the object of the game is very simple: just move one or more fish from the high-tide line to the sandpail on mommy's beach blanket.

Player Assignments

Tackles

The littlest players get this job. Their assignment is to nosedive into the soggy sand and grab the fish with both hands. This is an excellent choice for kids under five, since it's exactly what they'll wind up doing anyway.

Halfback

At halftime, you can promote your best tackle to halfback, provided he let only half the fish he caught slip through his hands and return to the ocean. If the less successful players get jealous, you can promote them to *quarterbacks*.

Tailback

When two players dispute possession of the fish, one brings the head back with most of the rest still attached. The other will probably stop crying if you make him the Star Tailback.

Running Back

There's one in every crowd. He (or she) hates getting wet, won't touch the fish, complains about the other players, cries a lot, and sooner or later goes running back to . . .

The Coach

This job is usually reserved for daddies. The coach sits on the sidelines, drinks beer and keeps an eye on the chaos. He's responsible for making sure the halfback doesn't hit the running back with anything bigger than a wet fish. He may yell and exhort his players to "go get those fish over there and stop kicking your brother." And he must provide inspiration for soggy tailbacks who drip on his beach blanket and insist on sitting on his lap. When the coach gets possession of a fish, he passes it off to . . .

The Mommy

She cleans the fish, cleans the kids and gets the running back to stop throwing sand at her brother. After the game, she carries unconscious players from the car to their bedrooms, where she changes them into their jammies without waking them up.

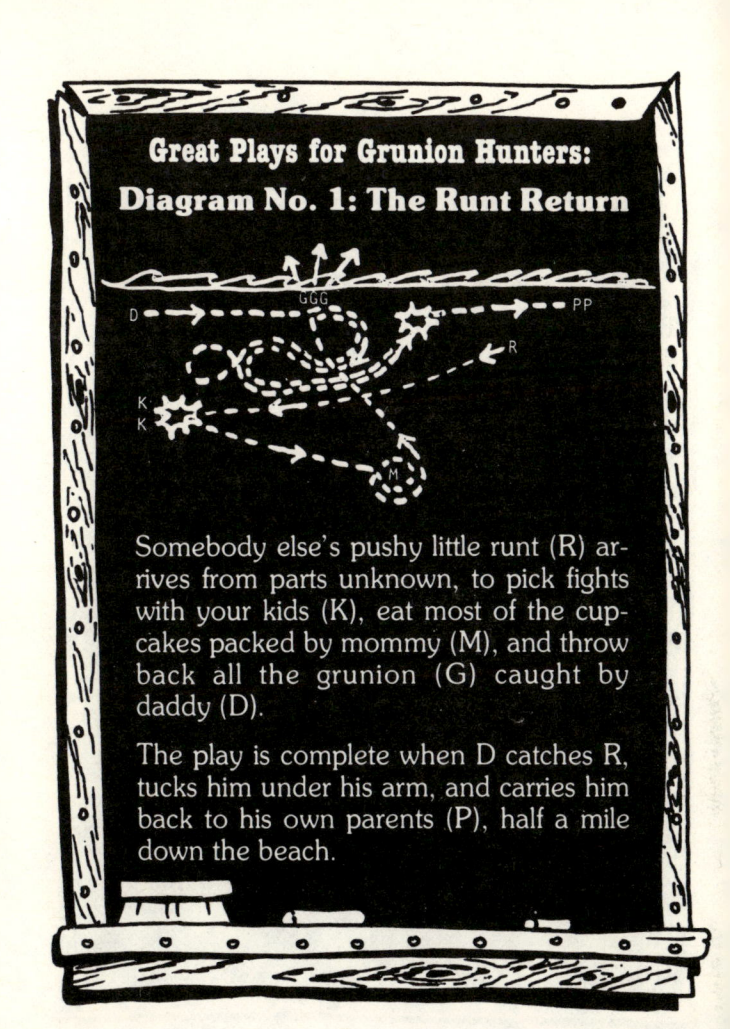

Great Plays for Grunion Hunters:
Diagram No. 1: The Runt Return

Somebody else's pushy little runt (R) arrives from parts unknown, to pick fights with your kids (K), eat most of the cupcakes packed by mommy (M), and throw back all the grunion (G) caught by daddy (D).

The play is complete when D catches R, tucks him under his arm, and carries him back to his own parents (P), half a mile down the beach.

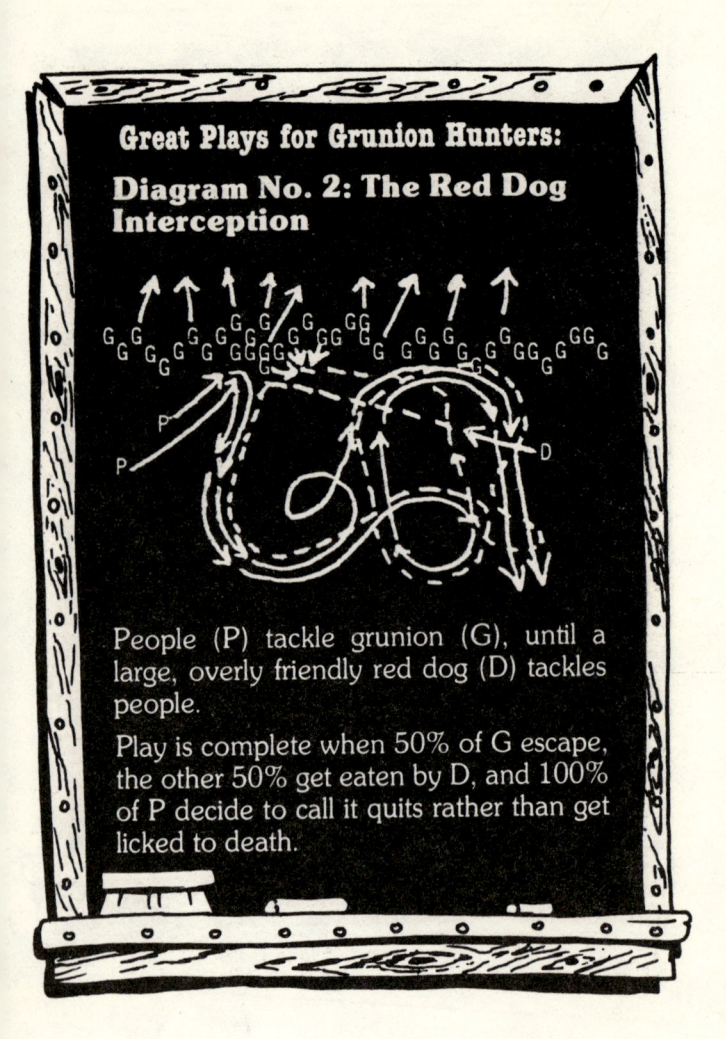

Great Plays for Grunion Hunters:

Diagram No. 2: The Red Dog Interception

People (P) tackle grunion (G), until a large, overly friendly red dog (D) tackles people.

Play is complete when 50% of G escape, the other 50% get eaten by D, and 100% of P decide to call it quits rather than get licked to death.

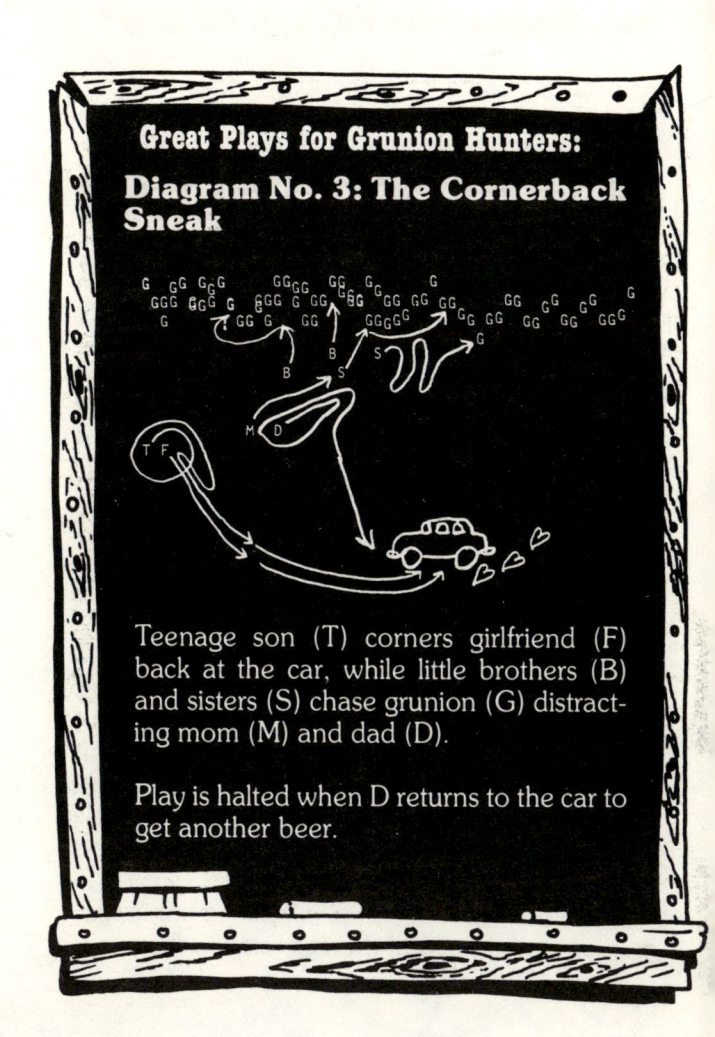

Great Plays for Grunion Hunters:

Diagram No. 3: The Cornerback Sneak

Teenage son (T) corners girlfriend (F) back at the car, while little brothers (B) and sisters (S) chase grunion (G) distracting mom (M) and dad (D).

Play is halted when D returns to the car to get another beer.

What Happens to the Fish That Get Away?

A lot of people have the wrong idea. Salmon may die after spawning, but grunion don't. With luck, a grunion will live three years, sometimes longer, and spawn at least four times per year. So the fish you *almost* caught may produce thousands of grunion that you can *almost* catch in years to come.

That brings us to an important point: If you don't plan to eat them, please throw them back! If you won't do it for the grunion's sake, do it for future grunion hunters who deserve the chance to have the same fun you did. Grunion populations seem to have fallen off in the past few years. A little caution right now could help prevent bigger problems in later years. Grunion are unique— and irreplaceable.

That doesn't mean you shouldn't catch grunion. The number you take for food won't endanger them. But nature doesn't owe you a year's supply of cat food, or free fertilizer for your garden. And taking grunion, only to discard them in the parking lot, is wasteful. Grunion may be funny. But even funny fish deserve some respect. If we behave irresponsibly and waste nature's blessings, we lose them. It's happened before, too many times.

When the run is over, the people go home, the grunion go home, and the eggs stay in the sand.

As mommy and daddy swim away, the receding waves dump a few extra inches of sand on top of the eggs, insulating them so they'll have just the right amount of heat and moisture.

That's why grunion can only spawn during certain months and at certain phases of the tidal cycle. The eggs must stay undisturbed in their sandy incubator for at least nine or ten days. And by no coincidence, it'll be ten to thirteen days before the rising tide loosens the sand on top of them. Then, like the doctor's spank on a baby's backside, the waves smack the eggs with a cold, saltwater shower to tell them that it's time to get cracking. And crack they do. Within seconds, all two or three thousand of them explode from their shells "like popcorn."

But some high tides are a lot higher than others. And if the eggs were laid after a very high tide, the next one probably won't be high enough to reach them. That sounds like a fatal problem, but it isn't. The eggs contain enough food to keep the babies alive for another two weeks. Much longer than 30 days and they'll be goners, but that rarely happens.

Baby grunion are immediately able to fend for themselves. They dine on micro-organisms and grow—*fast*. When they hatch, they're barely big enough to see. But in a year, they'll be five inches long and ready to spawn.

Cooking Your Catch

The simplest method I found for preparing grunion came from a nine-year-old La Jolla girl. She suggested we "just give them to the maid." So I asked the maid how she fixed grunion. She had a secret recipe: Feed the grunion to the cat and buy something at the fish market that's already boned and cleaned. The kid was too dumb to notice the difference and the parents were too smart to mention it.

That brings us to an important point. Grunion aren't the best-tasting fish in the world. Generally, any recipe that works with smelt will work with grunion. But grunion aren't smelt and their flavor isn't as good. So don't expect the same results.

Some people just cut off the heads and tails, wipe them with a slightly damp cloth to remove the slippery substance their skins secrete, and dump them into a frying pan full of oil. People who like them that way fall into a special category: hungry. And adult.

Let's not kid ourselves. There's no way your seven-year-old girl, who turns up her nose at milk that has a speck in it, is going to eat a fish with bones and skin. So if you want your little grunion hunters to actually eat what they catch, you're in for a bit of work.

Start by cutting off the head and tail. Then slice off the fins and split the fish down the top and bottom. Break it open to remove the entrails and pull out the bone. Then take a small piece of cloth (to improve your grip) and pull off the skin. You now have two filets—enough for most people, since most people don't like grunion. But an adult who *does* like grunion will easily eat a dozen filets. For all that effort, they're not very big.

Melt some butter in a large frying pan, until you have ⅛ inch or more. (Butter is best for flavor, but it burns easily. Cooking oil is easier to handle, but doesn't have the flavor. So I mix them, 50–50.)

Salt and pepper the filets to taste, then roll them in flour. Toss them into the pan and let them fry. A minute on each side is usually sufficient for me, but I guess that depends on the heat of your frying pan. Be careful of overcrowding the pan, since that results in uneven cooking. And keep in mind that the most common mistake in cooking fish is overcooking them. Good chefs seem to put fish into the same category as eggs: a little cooking does wonders, but a little too much is disastrous.

And Now, a Word From Our Spawn-sor...

By Nancy Margaret Moffatt Ph.D.

In recent years, heavy grunion runs in Southern California have been rare, even during peak spawning months. We don't know why. It could even be a natural cycle, but we know too little about the grunion to be sure. We don't know how many breeding populations there are. We aren't sure where they hang out during the "off" season. We don't even understand how they know when and where to spawn. And our lack of knowledge could prove disastrous for the grunion.

They've been in trouble before. In the 1920's, California had no laws to protect the grunion. Greedy grunion hunters stalked the beaches, using beach seines to catch them by the thousands. Finally, their numbers dipped so low that legislation was passed. March and April were closed. Fishing licenses and hand capture were required, and a limit of ten fish per person was set. But the law was only a limited success because it wasn't based on knowledge. Finally, research showed that the peak spawning months were April and May, not March and April. The closed months were changed, and only then did grunion populations recover.

It's an important lesson in conservation: blind stabs are rarely effective and can potentially do more harm than good. Intelligent management isn't possible without sound, basic research, and there just hasn't been enough of that to tell us whether the grunion is threatened or not.

Longtime grunion fans seem to agree that "there just aren't as many good runs these days." That's all we have to go on because no surveys have been done to establish what the normal numbers of grunion are, or measure the decline—if it really is a decline. Grunion aren't on any official "endangered species" list. Hopefully, they shouldn't be. But for lack of any better evidence, we must be forewarned. The grunion could be headed for an irreparable decline.

Why would that happen? One possible suspect is our disruption of the natural sand movements. Jetties, breakwaters, marinas and other structures are leaving many beaches virtually devoid of sand during the spring and summer months. Grunion can't spawn on cobbles and neither can people—sunbathe, that is. Because of the threat to the tourist trade, there may be some hue and cry about the sand loss. And since a lot of money is at stake, maybe we'll see our beautiful grunion and sunbathing beaches saved. Then all we'll have to worry about are chemical and thermal pollution, coastal development and similar all-purpose environmental headaches.

Actually, it's far from hopeless. People *can* learn, and have in the past. Once, grunion eggs were destroyed, wholesale, by the big tractor-drawn sand rakes that clean our beaches. But maintenance people were willing to learn. Now they rake less often during the spawning months and try to avoid killing the grunion eggs. A little knowledge can do wonders—but only if it comes in time.

For another interesting fish, the totoaba (sometimes called totoava), knowledge seems to have come too late. These big, handsome fish (up to six feet long and nearly 300 pounds) are considered by many to be the most delectable seafood of all. But they're only found in the Gulf of California, and for many years, fishing was done carelessly and wastefully.

Until the mid-1920's, the totoaba was exploited for its gas bladder, which was dried and exported to the Orient for use in soups. Beginning in 1926, Americans discovered that the rest of the totoaba was delicious, too, and fish were exported to the U.S. Annual yield increased rapidly until 1942. Then it began to decline. By the mid-1950's, the catch had dropped by about 65 percent. The Mexican government instituted a closed season and designated the area around the mouth of the Colorado River as a sanctuary. Their management measures were based strictly on folklore which said that the fish spawned in the fresh water of the river. Luckily, this was one case when folklore turned out to be right.

Still, by 1966–67, the totoaba catch had recovered to only about half of its 1942 peak. And after that, it dropped to an all-time low in 1975. Finally, the Mexican government prohibited all fishing for totoaba, in hopes of saving them from complete extinction. But the chance of that is very slim. Apart from the disastrous, unmanaged fishing, the totoaba faces another threat which will probably not be corrected: damming of the Colorado River has virtually eliminated the totoaba's spawning grounds. The fate of the totoaba since 1975 is a mystery. And if the population were miraculously to recover, we still wouldn't know enough to manage fishing properly. Now that's frustrating.

The Gulf grunion aren't faring much better. Even today, no Mexican laws protect them. Their spawning beaches are torn up by dune buggy tires which remove the sand from above the eggs, leaving them to die from exposure to the hot, dry air. I've even had the misfortune of seeing dune buggy drivers—Americans, of course—intentionally running over thousands of spawning grunion.

The grunions offer enough mysteries for a lifetime or two of research. But like everything else, grunion research costs money. There's a lot of competition for our inflation-ridden government's research funds, and learning about a fish that has no direct commercial value doesn't rate a very high priority.

Still, there are important lessons to be learned from the grunions and totoaba. Their environments are changing so fast that they can't adapt. Can we adapt any faster?

Too often, man's activities have needlessly led plants and animals to extinction. Certainly species have been going extinct for billions of years. But not this fast. And most of those extinctions weren't by conscious decision. They happened because we didn't think or didn't know.

We should think about these things, and weigh the consequences against the benefits. After all, do we miss the passenger pigeon? Will we miss the condor? The bald eagle? The totoaba? The snail darter? Is a species value tied only to its direct benefit to humans? Every species (including ours) is a piece of a larger picture. The loss of any species leaves a void. And since no two species are ecologically identical, that void can't be completely filled when the extinction process is so rapid. The result is an imbalance and a potential loss of efficiency in the natural systems which supply our food and energy.

The value of the totoaba can be measured by its table appeal and its limited geographic distribution. The grunion's value can be measured by its crazy method of reproduction, which is unique and absolutely fascinating to watch. But what about the snail darter, whose only claim to fame is that it's found in only one place, which happens to be directly in the way of the Tellico Dam? Had basic and seemingly pointless research been done before the dam site was chosen, maybe the problem could've been thought through in advance, and resolved. Ultimately, in the realm of the true sciences, there's no such thing as useless knowledge.

That's true at all levels of knowledge. The foundation is laid at the basic research level. But it doesn't stop there. Today, children and adults are more aware of the world around them. They have at least some understanding of problems like overpopulation, limited resources, the damage that unchecked development can do, the potential dangers of pollution. And they like being in the know. If I explain to tidepool tourists that rocks should be replaced as found, because tidepool creatures will die without their protective cover, they always cooperate. And I think they often pass the knowledge along.

So now that you've read Mike's book, you can do the same. When you go out after grunion, you'll have a lot of information to share with other grunion hunters. You don't need to be an expert to share your knowledge of grunion, and to let others know that without care they could become endangered. Lots of people catch grunion without intending to eat them. They might have more fun if someone showed them how to enjoy just watching. And you can do that. Conservation doesn't need fanatics. But people who care, and share their love of the natural world, play a very important role in preserving the good things in life.

And if you want to do more for the grunion, you can. Besides passing along the knowledge we already have about them, you can help find new knowledge by reporting the grunion runs you witness. We don't know yet what's happening to the grunion—whether they really are in a state of decline, and if they are, how fast this is happening. The only way to know is to observe and gather necessary information.

The form on the next two pages will tell you what to watch for. Run it off on a copier if you don't want to tear up your book. Or write me or Captain Mike and we'll send you some loose forms. Take the form along next time you go out to watch the grunion, and answer as many questions as you can. The starred questions are especially important. And if you go to the beach on the night of a predicted grunion run, and the grunion don't show up, that's data too. Send it in.

If everyone who reads this book became a grunion watcher, we could acquire a huge amount of data, very quickly. Serious gaps in our knowledge about grunion populations would be filled. Important questions could be answered.

Grunion Run Data Sheet

*Date: _____

Time of Arrival: _____ Departure: _____

*Location: (be as specific as possible, such as ½-mile south of Crystal Pier or in front of the Marine Room at La Jolla Shores) _____
_____

Approximately how much of the beach did you observe?
_____

Was a run predicted? Yes No If yes, at what time? _____

*Did the grunion run? Yes No

*If yes, give the time of:
  Start (first fish on beach): _____
  Middle (greatest number of fish on beach): _____
  End (last fish on beach): _____

*Intensity of run: (check one)
  Light (less than 10 fish per sq. yd.) _____
  Moderate (10 to 100 fish per sq. yd) _____
  Heavy (more than 100 fish per sq. yd.) _____

How many people were on the beach? _____

Were they taking fish? Yes No

And you could have the satisfaction of being a part of it. As far as I'm concerned, that beats a grunion dinner any day of the week.

So don't be a grunion hunter (unless you're actually hungry). Be a grunion watcher—and send in a data sheet as soon as you can.

—Nancy M. Moffatt, Ph.D.

If yes, did they seem to be aware of and abiding by the laws? Yes No

Did you approach and inform them about the grunion? Yes No

If yes, how many did you talk to? _____

Did you see any California Fish and Game Wardens?
Yes No

How many people were in your party? _____

Have you seen grunion here before? _____

Comments: _____
_____

Check here if you require more data sheets: _____

*Witness or witnesses: _____

*Address: _____
_____

Phone: _____

Mail To: Grunion Watch
   820 Palm Terrace
   Escondido, California 92025

*This information is especially important.

About the Author

"Captain" Mike Ambrose is San Diego's most popular TV weather reporter. He attempts to predict the unpredictable ten times a week, on the 5:00 and 11:00 p.m. editions of KGTV Channel 10's news. Sometimes he succeeds.

The title "Captain" is purely honorary. Mike was never in the military—a fact for which the military has never seemed properly grateful. However, he did once captain an outboard motorboat. (He would've captained it twice if it hadn't sunk.)

Mike has been grunion hunting many times, and has been directly responsible for the demise of three innocent little fish, so far. (Two of them were given to him by an eight-year-old girl who made some sort of remark about hating to see a grown man cry.) But because he hates to be wet, cold, covered with sand and/or out of breath, Mike has had a chance to watch some of the great grunion hunters in action.

This is Mike's first book. In spite of popular request, it may not be his last.

About the Other Culprits

Nora Scott Walker is a writer who makes TV spots to promote shows on KGTV. When she grows up, she hopes to become the literary counterpart of her longtime movie idol, Mickey Mouse. And it looks like she might make it.

Johnny Hawk is an unemployed falconer. When he's not busy with his bird, he spends his leisure time drawing pictures of Russian planes. But the Russians won't pay for them, so he sells them to the U.S. Navy. The drawings help pilots learn to recognize Soviet planes, and if any of those things come flying around here, the Navy wants to be the first to know.

Nancy Margaret Moffatt is a marine biologist who doesn't mind working with fishy characters. She got her Ph.D. from the University of Arizona for her research on Gulf grunion. She's crazy about grunion, but never eats them. After dissecting so many, she tends to lose her appetite the moment she sees one.

To purchase additional copies of
**Captain Mike's
Complete Guide to Grunion Hunting,**
please contact your local bookstore.

However, if you are unable to locate the
book in your area, copies may be ordered
from the publisher at the address below.

Copies are $3.95 each (plus a shipping
and handling charge of 75 cents for the
first book and 25 cents for each
additional copy.)

Oak Tree Publications, Inc.
11175 Flintkote Avenue, Suite CM
San Diego, CA 92121